EXTREME SUMMER
SPORTS ZONE

SKATEBOARDING VERT

Patrick G. Cain

Lerner Publications Company • Minneapolis

Lerner Publications Company
A division of Lerner Publishing Group, Inc.
241 First Avenue North
Minneapolis, MN 55401 U.S.A.
Website address: www.lernerbooks.com

Content Consultant: Jorge Angel, Skatepark of Tampa Event Coordinator

Library of Congress Cataloging-in-Publication Data

Cain, Patrick G.
    Skateboarding vert / by Patrick G. Cain.
        p.   cm. — (Extreme summer sports zone)
    Includes index.
    ISBN 978–1–4677–0748–0 (lib. bdg. : alk. paper)
    1. Skateboarding—Juvenile literature. I. Title.
GV859.8.C35 2013
796.22--dc23   2012027293

Manufactured in the United States of America
1 – BP – 12/31/12

The images in this book are used with the permission of: Backgrounds: © Grant Hindsley/AP Images, 5; © Guillermo Trejos/iStockphoto, 6; © Jeff Gross/Getty Images, 7; © AP Images, 8; © Focus on Sport/Getty Images, 9; © Steve Grayson/WireImage/Getty Images, 10; © Luciana Ellington/ Shutterstock Images, 11; © Alberto E. Rodriguez/Getty Images, 12; © Ahmad Faizal Yahya/ Shutterstock Images, 13; © Gerry Boughan/iStockphoto, 14; © Christian Pondella/Getty Images, 15; © Rob Marmion/Shutterstock Images, 16; © Mark J. Terrill/AP Images, 17, 24; © Stephen Gibson/ Shutterstock Images, 18; © AMA/Shutterstock Images, 19; © Kevork Djansezian/Getty Images, 20; © Mark R. Sullivan/AP Images, 21; © iStockphoto, 22; © Mat Szwajkos/Getty Images, 23; © Bret Hartman/AP Images, 25; © Julio Cesar Guimaraes/LatinContent/Getty Images, 26; © Harry How/ Getty Images, 27; © A. Einsiedler/Shutterstock Images, 28; © Rick Becker-Leckrone/Shutterstock, 29

Front cover: © Jeff Gross/Getty Images; © RTimages/Shutterstock.com (background).

Main body text set in Folio Std Light 11/17.
Typeface provided by Adobe Systems.

TABLE OF CONTENTS

CHAPTER ONE

WHAT IS SKATEBOARDING VERT?

In 2012 12-year-old Tom Schaar made history in the world of vertical (vert) skateboarding. The boy from Malibu, California, landed the first-ever 1080 spin on a skateboard. He sped up a ramp and rotated three times in the air before landing. The trick impressed professional skateboarders around the world. Every year fans watched their heroes do awesome vert tricks at the X Games. Tom proved that kids and amateurs were also pushing the limits of vert. And they were doing it in their own backyards.

TOM SCHAAR

Tom is a rising star in the vert world. Unlike most vert tricks, Tom's 1080 was not done on a half-pipe ramp. Instead, he used a 70-foot-high (21-meter) MegaRamp with a 27-foot-high (8-m) quarter pipe. In 2012 he made his first appearance at the X Games. He competed in both the skateboarding vert and big air events. While he did not land a 1080, he successfully landed a 900. His final score of 89.33 out of 100 earned him sixth place in the big air event. He took seventh place in the vert event.

Young skater
Tom Schaar
warms up before
the 2012 X Games
big air event.

Kids around the world have helped to make skateboarding one of the most popular action sports.

Kids first skateboarded in the streets, on sidewalks, and in parks. In the 1970s, a drought on the West Coast left a lot of swimming pools empty. Daring kids began using the pools' walls to do tricks. These kids used the curved drops of the inground pools as ramps. They built up speed to go higher and higher. Sometimes they caught air (got airborne). Without knowing it, these kids had invented a new sport: vert skateboarding.

What started as kids fooling around in their backyard pools became one of the biggest trends in sports. Vert skateboarder Tony Hawk went from unknown California beach boy to international

Since 1995 ESPN has held an action sports competition called the Extreme Games, shortened to X Games. It is the most important competition for extreme action sports. Like the Olympic Games, winners earn gold, silver, or bronze medals. X Games athletes also win prize money. Pro riders typically work for months, if not all year, trying to perfect a specific move. The X Games is often the birthplace for many never-before-seen tricks.

star. He quickly became a successful businessman. Skateboarding's huge popularity helped create major events such as the X Games.

Skateboarding and its vert events changed the extreme sports world forever. Young and talented riders like Tom keep catching bigger air (making bigger jumps). They continue inventing new tricks. Vert skateboarding is here to stay.

Pierre-Luc Gagnon won the gold medal at the 2012 X Games.

CHAPTER TWO

VERT'S BEGINNINGS

Vert skateboarding has changed a lot since the sport's early days.

Skateboarding had nothing to do with big air in its early days. In the early 1950s, kids attached roller-skate wheels to a board. This skateboard was very wobbly. By this time, surfing had been popular for years. But not everyone lived near an ocean. Surfers and surfing fans took the sport to land. The first commercial skateboard was sold in 1959.

Early vert skaters used empty pools as ramps.

These early skateboards had metal wheels. Later, they were replaced with clay wheels. Skateboarding took off as a sport. In 1963 the first skateboard competition was held. But kids were still skating in streets and on sidewalks.

Then came the drought of the 1970s. Lots of houses in Southern California had inground pools. People had to save water. Pool owners weren't allowed to fill the pools. When pools dried up, young skateboarders found a new use for them. They used the pool walls as ramps. By that time, skateboards had polyurethane wheels. This tough material created good traction. The wheels also didn't break as easily as clay wheels did. Skateboarders could try trickier moves without slipping or damaging their boards. The magazine *SkateBoarder* told the world about this new way to ride.

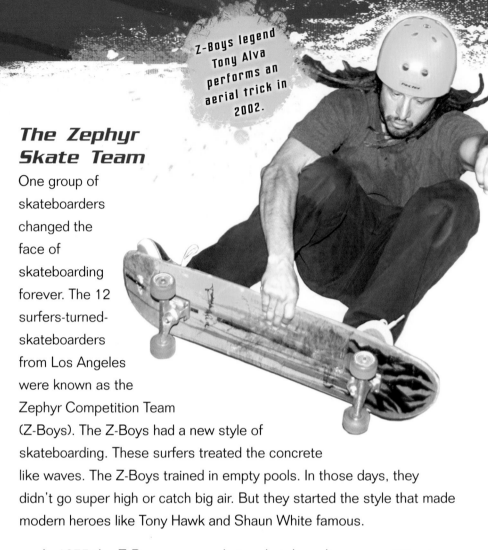

The Zephyr Skate Team

One group of skateboarders changed the face of skateboarding forever. The 12 surfers-turned-skateboarders from Los Angeles were known as the Zephyr Competition Team (Z-Boys). The Z-Boys had a new style of skateboarding. These surfers treated the concrete like waves. The Z-Boys trained in empty pools. In those days, they didn't go super high or catch big air. But they started the style that made modern heroes like Tony Hawk and Shaun White famous.

In 1975 the Z-Boys appeared at a skateboarding competition in Del Mar, California. Their edgy moves showed off their rebellious attitudes. Major sponsors quickly scooped up the members of the team. The Z-Boys had taken the skateboarding world by storm. Soon skateboarders were performing Z-Boys' tricks off of half-pipe ramps. Unlike the empty pools, the half-pipe ramps were perfectly smooth. The tricks could be bigger. Modern vert skateboarding had arrived.

THE HALF PIPE

Tom Stewart created the first half pipe in 1975. Stewart was a teen rider living in California. He took the design from large water pipes used in the Arizona desert. With the help of his older brother, Tom built a wooden half pipe in his yard. The design was an instant success. Tom soon started a business called Rampage to sell the ramp to others. The half pipe quickly became an important part of many action sports. Half-pipe events are a big part of BMX biking, snowboarding, and other events.

Vert skaters use a half-pipe ramp for many of their tricks.

A New Shoe

After the Z-Boys split up, young riders such as Tony Hawk and Steve Caballero continued pushing the limits. To do more extreme tricks, they needed better equipment. Skateboards themselves hadn't changed much since the sport's early days. The biggest change in skateboarding technology came in the skateboarders' shoes. Skaters in the early 1980s had major problems with their shoes. The rubber on the bottom wore out quickly. The daring moves the skaters did damaged their laces.

Peggy Oki (center) was the only woman on the Zephyr Team. Nathan Pratt (left) and Paul Constantineau (right) also skated with the Z-Boys.

Vert shoes need to be sturdy enough to handle daring tricks and hard falls.

Mac Mann was an 11-year-old boy who loved to skateboard. He sometimes watched Tony Hawk practice in Del Mar. Mac often had to replace his skateboarding shoes. Mac's father, Bill Mann, designed shoes for a living. Mac suggested that his dad make a shoe built especially for skateboarding. Bill Mann designed a new, sturdy sneaker built to hold up to extreme tricks. Mac suggested they call the shoe Airwalk after one of Hawk's most famous moves. The Airwalk shoe was an instant success. It changed the way skateboarders rode. It increased the tricks they could do. The Airwalk brand eventually sponsored many pro skateboarders.

CHAPTER THREE

SKATEBOARDING BRANDS, EQUIPMENT, AND MOVES

Having the right equipment is a key part of skateboarding. Skateboarding gear is a huge part of the sport. A relaxed clothing style comes along with the gear. This style has helped give skateboarding its own culture. Major brands such as Vans, etnies, DC, and Nike create gear for skateboarders. They model their clothing and gear on what skateboarders are already wearing and using. Skateboarding brands also sponsor skaters from around the world.

Most vert skaters wear comfortable clothing so they can move easily. Although not all skaters wear helmets and pads, it's a good idea to wear them.

Sponsors are an important part of vert skateboarding. DC and Red Bull are two companies that sponsor Tom Schaar (right).

Getting Sponsored

Getting sponsored is a huge deal for an amateur skateboarder hoping to go pro. The sport may have never gone mainstream without brands to sponsor vert skaters. Being a pro vert skateboarder is a full-time job. It requires a ton of practice. Sponsors financially support skateboarders so they can spend their time perfecting new tricks.

Companies such as ESPN, Red Bull, and Mountain Dew sponsor extreme sports competitions featuring vert skateboarding. They bring adventurous vert skaters and their awesome tricks to new audiences. People around the world can watch these pros compete on television and online.

Vert skateboarding can be a dangerous sport. Skaters wear helmets and pads so they can get back on their boards after hard falls.

Safety

To keep getting better, a vert skateboarder needs to prevent injuries. Safety is the most important part of vert. Learning new tricks means taking hard falls. Even X Games vert skaters are required to wear helmets when competing. Accidents are very dangerous. Bad falls can cost skaters their careers. If a pro gets a serious injury and can't skate, that skater might lose sponsors and not make money. According to the pros, here are three must-haves to stay safe:

Helmet: A helmet is a good idea no matter what a skater's skill level is. Most pro skateboarders use bowl helmets with a hard

plastic outer material. These helmets often have different colors and patterns. A skater's helmet can be just as expressive as the skater's vert tricks.

Knee pads: Many vert skaters fall by sliding down the half pipe on their knees. Pro skaters know landing on their knee pads is one of the safest ways to take a spill.

Elbow pads: A skater's reflexes kick in when taking a spill. The skater usually extends his or her arms to break the fall. Without elbow pads, a skater can get serious arm injuries.

BREAKDOWN OF A SKATEBOARD

WHEELS

The wheels were one of the first major changes made to skateboards. If a wheel breaks or falls off during a trick, a skater could be seriously injured. The sturdy, polyurethane wheels on most skateboards let skaters ride smoothly on different surfaces. Vert skaters prefer bigger wheels than street skateboarders.

TRUCKS

The trucks are the metal pieces connecting the board to the wheels. A skateboard's trucks allow riders to lean on the deck's sides. This makes the deck tilt. The tilt allows the skateboard to make smooth turns. Trucks come in different sizes based on the size of the deck. A wider truck makes it easier to turn. A narrower truck makes it easier for the skater to do flip tricks.

DECK

A skateboard's deck may look basic. But it is more than just a piece of wood with curved ends. A skateboard needs to be very tough to hold up to all the moves a skater puts it through. The board also needs to be flexible so a rider can move it. Skateboard makers often use seven layers of wood when making the deck. Decks come in many shapes and sizes. Vert skateboarders usually prefer a wider board.

GRIP TAPE

Grip tape is the sandpaper-like material on skateboard decks. This gritty surface gives skaters traction on their boards. Skaters can lean more deeply and land tricks more easily if their feet are not slipping off the decks.

Grabs can be combined with other tricks. Some athletes choose to not wear safety gear. But safety gear is always a good idea. One bad fall can lead to a serious injury.

The Moves

Vert skateboarding features many different tricks and moves. Skaters combine individual tricks to create more advanced tricks called combos. Skateboarding vert is all about aerial moves. These moves can be tough. The falls can be hard. The only way to master these tricks is with tons of practice. Here are a few of the moves you might see pro riders pulling off during competitions:

Grab

A skater does a grab any time he or she reaches down to hold on to the board. Skaters often use grabs as part of combos.

Aerial Spin

Numbers such as 360, 540, 720, or 900 measure aerial spins. The numbers represent the degrees of the turn. A 360 is when a rider uses the half pipe to spin one full time. A 540 is one and a half spins. A 720 is two full spins. And a 900 is two and a half spins. The 1080 Tom Schaar pulled in 2012 was three full spins.

Invert

In an invert, the skater approaches the lip of the half pipe and places a hand on the ramp. The board comes over the skater's head. Then the skater is able to rotate and plant the board back on the ramp. A skater can do an invert in many different ways.

Bucky Lasek does an invert at the 2003 Mountain Dew National Championships.

Backside Kick Turn

The backside kick turn is a common trick for beginning vert skaters. The skater approaches the top of the ramp and lets the nose (front) of the board come off the ramp. The skater then turns the board around. The backside kick turn is a building block for many bigger tricks.

Backside Nose-Grab Turn

The backside nose-grab turn is a backside kick turn with a grab added on to it. As the nose of the board comes off the ramp, the skater reaches down to grab the nose. Some skaters add to this trick by including a slight lift. They catch air as they turn around.

Backside Air

A backside air begins with a backside nose grab turn. The skater adds more air to the turn by pulling the skateboard toward his or her body.

Many pros catch air in a backside nose-grab turn.

The backside air is a common trick in vert skateboarding.

Airwalk

An airwalk is a no-footed version of the backside air. When catching air on the half pipe, the skater grabs onto the nose of the board and removes both feet from the board. Then the skater plants the feet back on the board before landing. Tony Hawk was the first skater to do this move on a vert ramp.

TONY HAWK

Many fans see Hawk as the most influential skater in vert history. He started skating when he was nine years old. He started winning amateur contests in California when he was only 12. By the age of 14, he was a pro skater. In 1999 Hawk landed the first 900-degree spin. The move shocked the world. But it isn't just Hawk's moves that make him so influential. He is also a talented businessman. He has marketed his sport to kids and adults. From the mid-1980s to the 2000s, he appeared in skate videos and documentaries. The videos show viewers awesome stunts. Rookie skaters learn more about what it takes to be a pro. In 1999 he created the first of his 15 video games, *Tony Hawk's Pro Skater*.

GOING PRO

Most skaters don't do tricks to earn money or fame. Most skaters skateboard because they love to skate. They show off their moves to their friends and families. They challenge themselves with new moves. But with enough hard work, a skater might become good enough to enter an amateur competition. At the competition, a sponsor or a team may notice a talented skater. When a team or a company offers to sponsor a skater, he or she may be able to ride professionally. Some skaters represent a brand as an amateur for a few years before going pro.

Team Riding

Professional skateboarders often skate in teams.

Canadian skater Pierre-Luc Gagnon competes in the 2004 X Games vert competition. Vert skateboarders compete as individuals.

Skateboard teams are different from teams in sports such as basketball. Being on a team means all the skaters on that team are paid by the same sponsor. But skateboarders are judged individually. Teammates will often compete against one another at the same events.

Shaun White won the gold medal at the 2011 X Games vert competition.

SHAUN WHITE

Many fans see Shaun White as the next Tony Hawk. When White skates, he dominates. White's skill was obvious from a young age. Tony Hawk first saw Shaun when he was nine years old and became his mentor. Hawk helped White become a pro when White turned 16. White has since won two gold medals in the X Games for skateboarding vert. Like Hawk, White has video games and successful businesses. But White isn't only known for his vert skateboarding skills. He is also a superstar snowboarder. He has won two Olympic gold medals in the snowboarding half pipe.

Competitions around the world bring pros together.

What Are the Events?

Skateboarding vert doesn't have a regular season like football or baseball. But several vert events throughout the year bring together the best pro skaters from around the world. Red Bull sponsors several competitions. Mountain Dew hosts the Dew Tour. For most fans, the biggest vert event of the year is the summer ESPN X Games. The X Games air on ESPN and ABC television. Only the very best vert riders compete in the X Games.

LYN-Z ADAMS HAWKINS PASTRANA

Lyn-z Adams Hawkins Pastrana is a skateboarding superstar. She grew up in Southern California where she learned to surf. She started skateboarding when she was six years old. Since then she has taken the skateboarding world by storm. In 2009 she was the first woman to land a 540. She competed in all but one X Games women's vert event. She has won eight X Games medals, including three golds.

Lyn-z Adams Hawkins Pastrana won the gold medal in the women's vert event at the 2009 X Games.

What's Winning?

In a skateboarding vert competition, skaters are judged on the difficulty of their moves and their style in doing their trick routine. If a skater makes his or her tricks as long and smooth as possible, that skater may earn a high score for style. The skater gets the chance to do several 30-second vert runs. In the 2012 X Games, each skater got five attempts. Each run is scored out of 100 points. The judges take the highest score. Pierre-Luc Gagnon is currently one of the best skaters in vert. In 2012 he won his sixth gold medal at the X Games.

Women's Vert

In 2003 the summer X Games added a women's vert event. The event was a huge victory for female skaters. It proved that they could compete at the same level as male skaters. Lyn-z Adams Hawkins Pastrana dominated women's vert. She won three gold medals. Brazilian skater Karen Jonz won four medals, including one gold in 2008. By 2010 the sport's popularity had begun declining. There were fewer competitors. In 2011 the X Games canceled the women's vert event. But that wasn't the end of women's skateboarding. Female skaters like Jonz and Hawkins Pastrana still skate vert ramps around the world. And women's skateboarding street is still a hugely popular X Games event.

Brazilian skater Karen Jonz is one of the top female vert skaters in the world.

Many amateur vert skaters film their tricks so the world can watch online.

Where to Watch

Television isn't the only place to check out amazing vert tricks. Thanks to video-sharing websites such as YouTube, many riders tape themselves doing tricks and post the videos online. If their tricks are really good, people will notice. Fans who don't want to wait for the competitions can have a parent or an adult help find skateboarding vert videos online. Beginning riders need to be careful, however. Trying to copy moves shown online can be a quick way to get injured!

GLOSSARY

AERIAL

in the air

AMATEUR

someone who participates in an activity for fun without expectation of payment

COMBO

a group of tricks done together

MAINSTREAM

something that is commonly accepted

MENTOR

an experienced skateboarder who helps a new skater learn the sport

PROFESSIONAL

someone who participates in an activity as a job for payment

ROOKIE

someone who is new to a sport or activity

SPONSOR

a company that financially supports professional athletes in a sport so they can focus on that sport

TRACTION

gripping power to keep a skater from slipping

FOR MORE INFORMATION

Further Reading

Braun, Eric. *Tony Hawk*. Minneapolis: Lerner Publications Company, 2004.

Cain, Patrick G. *Skateboarding Street*. Minneapolis: Lerner Publications Company, 2013.

Doeden, Matt. *Shaun White*. Minneapolis: Lerner Publications Company, 2011.

Powell, Ben. *Skateboarding*. Minneapolis: Lerner Publications Company, 2004.

Thomas, Isabel. *Board Sports*. Minneapolis: Lerner Publications Company, 2012.

Websites

ESPN X Games
http://espn.go.com/action/xgames
The official X Games website features information about the X Games. Check out skateboarding vert athlete bios, videos, and scores, and find out when and where the next X Games will be held.

KidsSkateboarding.net
http://kidsskateboarding.net/
This website features skateboarding tips, videos, safety information, and more especially for kids.

The Science of Skateboarding
http://www.kidzworld.com/article/5207-the-science-of-skateboarding
Learn more about the science behind skateboarding tricks, including how a half-pipe ramp helps a vert skater catch air.

INDEX

About the Author

Patrick Cain is a nuclear engineer turned writer. He is an award-winning journalist whose work often appears in a number of magazines such as *ESPN the Magazine*, and *Fast Company*. He currently lives in Los Angeles, California, but will forever be tied to upstate New York.